MY BIG NOTEBOOK OF *Ingenious* IDEAS!

KPLA Publishing

My Big Book of Ingenious Ideas!
ISBN 13 – 978-1-943833-24-5
ISBN 10 - 1-943833-24-9
Copyright 2017 © by KPLA Publishing; designed by Kimberly Millionaire

Published by:
KPLA Publishing – Kissed Publications
PO Box 9819
Hampton, VA 23670
www.kplapublishing.com

10 9 8 7 6 5 4 3 2 1

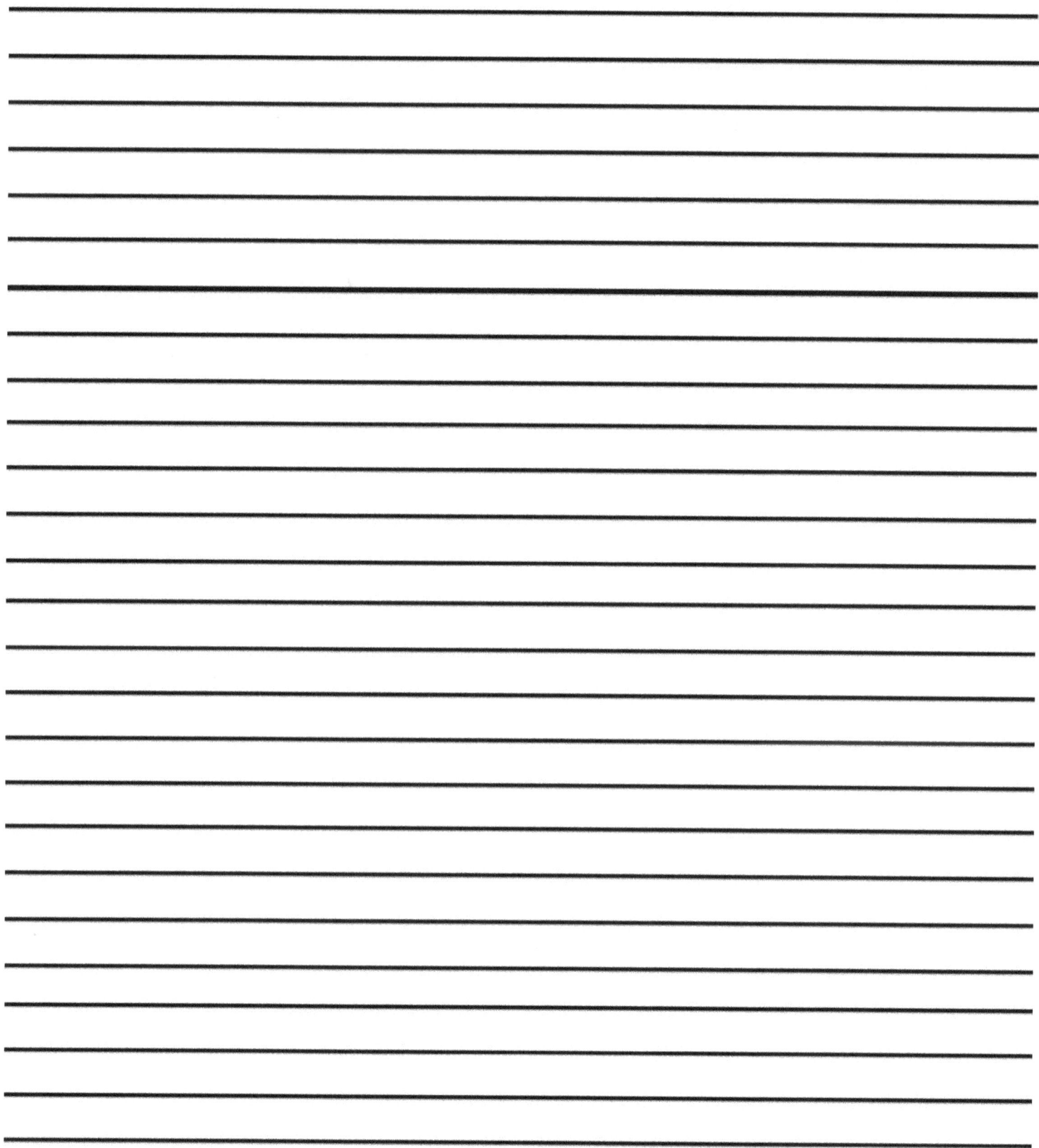

www.ingramcontent.com/pod-product-compliance
Lightning Source LLC
Chambersburg PA
CBHW081646270326
41933CB00018B/3368